# Table of Contents

# Navigating Generational Boundaries: Building Strong Relationships with Adult Children

*Recognizing the changing dynamics between parents and adult children and Understanding the desire for independence and the importance of setting boundaries*

**Edna Easter Hatfield**

# Dedication

This book is dedicated to my daughters Chloe, Madison, and Avery.

# Table of Contents

# Introduction

The strong, ever-evolving relationship between parents and their offspring transcends time and generations. The characteristics of these relationships change as children develop into adults, posing new difficulties and opportunities for both parties.

Parents must cross these generational divides with knowledge and empathy for today's culture where sociological and cultural changes have transformed the landscape of maturity. This requires an exploration of the evolving dynamics between parents and their adult children, placing special emphasis on the need to respect each other's limits and acknowledge the need for independence.

There are no longer rigid milestones that designate the passage from childhood to maturity and regulate the move into independence.

The time when parents provide financial support for young adults has been extended due to economic uncertainty, rising college tuition prices, and changing cultural beliefs. A new paradigm has developed, blurring the lines between childhood and maturity. This calls for a new way of looking at how parents can effectively maintain strong connections with their adult children.

To navigate these changing dynamics, it is crucial to grasp young adults' need for independence. They long to develop their own identities, make decisions that are in line with their interests and goals, and design their own life trajectories. Parents must appreciate and embrace this intrinsic desire for independence while still playing a supporting role that takes into account their adult children's need for direction and emotional support. Parents can establish the groundwork for a solid and mutually satisfying relationship with their adult children by striking a fine balance between empowerment and encouragement.

Setting limits is an essential component of creating strong connections with adult children, along with understanding independence. Boundaries serve as guiding principles that specify the roles, obligations, and demands placed on both parents and their grown children.

They give parents a framework to help their adult children while giving them the flexibility to live their own lives and gain wisdom from their experiences. Parents may effectively explain their boundaries and make sure that their adult children understand and respect them through open and transparent lines of communication. Similarly, adult children can share their wants, goals, and limitations, developing mutual understanding and a relationship based on respect and trust.

This book will dive into the societal and cultural trends that have contributed to prolonged parental support for young adults, as well as, begin the investigation of crossing generational barriers.

Research will show how economic developments have changed what it means to be an adult, how cultural shifts have redefined independence, and the importance of boundaries for creating and preserving successful relationships. Understanding these shifting dynamics will help parents arm themselves with the information and skills necessary to build solid, enduring relationships with their adult children.

Join me in exploring the challenges of developing trusting connections with adult children, accepting their need for independence, and appreciating the need for establishing boundaries. By accepting these ideas, parents can create strong, long-lasting relationships that cut through generational barriers and lay the groundwork for love, trust, and understanding between parents and their adult children.

# Chapter One

## Changing Dynamics

**Exploring the Societal and Cultural Shifts that have Led to Prolonged Parental Support for Young Adults.**

Long-term parental assistance for young adults has become a prominent and common phenomenon in recent years. The time when turning 18 meant becoming totally independent and self-reliant is long gone. Young adults today depend more and more on their parents for material, emotional, and practical support well into their 20s and beyond.

Let us examine the socioeconomic and cultural changes that have influenced this phenomenon and shed light on the variables affecting this extended parental assistance.

- **Employment and Education**

The evolving nature of education and job is one of the main causes of the prolonged parental support for young adults. In the past, obtaining a bachelor's degree or a high school diploma frequently ensured employment security.

However, young adults confront greater uncertainty and difficulties in finding meaningful employment in today's fiercely competitive job market. Additional education and training have been required as a result of rising college tuition prices, the need for specialized skills, and a changing employment market, which has increased the need for parental support.

Additionally, it has grown more difficult to make the transition from school to the workforce. The typical stepping stones for career growth now include internships, unpaid work, and in some cases studying abroad. Due to these situations, many young adults struggle financially and cannot fully support themselves; they must rely on parental help to pay for expenses like rent, bills, and even the most basic necessities.

### • Economic Conditions

Extended parental assistance for young adults has also been influenced by societal and economic changes. Young individuals have a hard time becoming financially independent due to economic changes including stagnant salaries and rising living expenses. The financial difficulties that young adults now confront are a result of factors such as inflation, rising housing costs, and the weight of student loan debt. For example, in 1995 a single-family home in the United States had a median cost of $163,000. In 2023, the median cost has soared to an astounding $437,000. As a result, parents frequently fill the gap and offer essential assistance to ensure their kids can handle the rigors of early adulthood.

### • Economic Elements

The economic environment is one of the key elements affecting the evolving relationships between parents and adult children. Young adults around the world must contend with a tightening labor market, rising living expenses, and fewer work options. They consequently frequently rely on their parents for financial assistance to support themselves.

In recent years, the price of almost everything has soared from grocery store items to buying a car. Significant loan debt is a common problem for young adults, which makes it harder for them to become financially independent. As a result, compared to past generations, parents now find themselves supporting their adult offspring for a longer amount of time.

### • Cultural Considerations

The dynamics between parents and adult children have changed significantly as a result of cultural changes. Since young adults today want to create their own identities and make their own decisions, they may diverge from their parents' ideal expectations. They pursue occupations and lifestyles that are in line with their interests and passions to achieve personal fulfillment.

Furthermore, society's expectations and conventions have evolved. Today's youth are urged to place a high priority on their own well-being, mental health, and personal development. Some cultures may express emotions openly and emphasize individualism, while others find it difficult to cope with stressful situations. If parents are not willing to be open minded about their adult children's interests and passions, this can lead them to have anxiety, depression, and feelings of isolation. When children are focusing on their own well-being, parents frequently need to provide continual assistance as their children make their way toward independence. Parental assistance can be as simple as encouraging adult children to follow their passions and praise them as they meet their individual goals.

# The impact of these changes on the parent-child relationship and the need to adapt to the new normal

In the past, the connection between parents and children was frequently characterized by a distinct power dynamic, with parents taking on an authoritative position and kids being expected to follow along. But in contemporary culture, there has been a shift toward a more egalitarian outlook, where kids are encouraged to express their thoughts and take part in decision-making. This modification represents an increased focus on children's autonomy, uniqueness, and development of their feeling of self-worth.

Parental duties have also changed as a result of changing economic and workplace factors. Parents are balancing more duties due to the development of dual-income homes, single-parent families, and non-traditional family configurations. This poses particular difficulties, such as juggling job and family obligations, making sure that children have enough time with their parents, and offering emotional support in a busy world.

### Effects of Technology

The way we interact and communicate has been completely transformed by technological breakthroughs. These developments present benefits for parent-child relationships that cannot be denied, such as rapid access to information and worldwide communication.

The widespread use of smartphones, social networking sites, and digital entertainment can produce a distracted environment that prevents parents and kids from having meaningful interactions.

Additionally, growing up in the digital age exposes kids to new dangers including cyberbullying, predators online, and the damaging effects of too much screen time on their mental and physical health. By actively participating in their children's digital life, establishing limits, and teaching them about responsible technology use, parents must be watchful and adjust to the new reality.

**Adapting to the New Normal**

First, as kids, parents must adjust to the new norm in order to deal with how societal and cultural changes affect the parent-child connection. In light of these modifications, consider the following tactics for fostering wholesome relationships:

- **Open Conversation:** Promote honest conversation with your kids by creating a safe space for them to share their ideas, worries, and feelings. Building trust and enhancing the parent-child relationship requires actively listening to children and recognizing their experiences.

- **Recognize that in Today's Varied Culture, a One-Size-Fits-All Strategy May Not be Effective.** As long as you continue to give your child direction, boundaries, and consistency, you can modify your parenting approach to suit their particular needs and temperament.

- **Technology Moderation:** Set reasonable screen time restrictions and encourage offline activities that foster social contact, physical activity, and creativity. To foster closer ties and quality time, take part in tech-free family activities.

- **Education and Awareness:** Keep up with the most recent developments, dangers, and difficulties facing contemporary society. Become informed on responsible technology use, internet safety, and the value of critical thinking in the digital age for both you and your kids.

- **Emphasize the Importance of Cultural Diversity:** Adopt an inclusive perspective in your family and emphasize the importance of cultural variety by encouraging exposure to other cultures. Participate in events that honor various customs, foods, and holidays. Encourage your kids to socialize with other kids who come from different backgrounds so that they can develop empathy and understanding.

- **In Order to Achieve a Healthy Work-Life Balance, Prioritize Spending Quality Time with Your Children.** Set aside time for family activities like game evenings, trips, and shared meals. Parent-child relationships can be boosted and enduring memories can be made by being completely present and involved during these occasions.

- **Lifelong Learning:** Adopt a growth-oriented attitude toward lifelong learning. Be receptive to fresh parenting concepts, viewpoints, and strategies. Maintain up-to-date knowledge of theories and methods in child development, parenting strategies, and new societal trends. This information can enable you to make wise choices and adjust to your children's evolving requirements.

- **Seek Community and Support:** Keep in mind that you are not going through these changes alone. Join parenting groups, look for support from other parents, or become involved in local events to meet people who share your interests and are dealing with the same issues. Sharing experiences, getting counsel, and establishing a support system can all offer insight and emotional assistance.

In essence, maintaining solid and healthy parent-child connections depends on adjusting to the new normal as socioeconomic and cultural changes continue to impact our world.

Parents can negotiate these changes and create a nurturing atmosphere that fosters growth by embracing open communication, being aware of technology's impact, supporting cultural diversity, and placing a priority on quality time.

The secret is to be open to change, to keep informed, and to be prepared to grow with your child. Always keep in mind that every family is different, so what works for one family may not work for another.

Amid a quickly changing society, parents may cultivate strong, enduring, and rewarding relationships with their children by continuing to learn, adapt, and stay connected.

As children enter adulthood, it's crucial to adjust to the new dynamics if you want to keep your relationship with them happy and healthy. The parent-child connection naturally changes as children mature and become adults.

In order to build a strong and respectful relationship with your adult children, parents must recognize and acknowledge these changes. Here are some important things to think about and things parents may do to adjust to the new dynamics:

• **Acknowledge the Change:** It is an important milestone when a parent-child relationship changes to an adult-adult relationship. Recognize that your child has grown into an independent person with their own ideas, beliefs, and values. The first step in adjusting to the shifting dynamic is accepting this transition.

• **Communication and Attentive Listening:** In any relationship, communication is key. It is even more important to encourage honest and open communication when your child grows older and becomes an adult. Encourage your child to communicate their thoughts and feelings, pay attention to what they have to say, and create a safe environment where they may do so without fear of being judged.

- **Respect Boundaries:** Honor the restrictions your adult child has set. They might have distinct expectations for their decision-making, personal space, and privacy. Recognize that their decisions might not be the same as yours and that it is crucial to promote their independence and uniqueness.

- **Provide Support, Not Direction:** Growing up typically entails accepting more responsibility and exercising autonomy. Instead of attempting to dictate or control their decisions, provide your support and direction when asked. Even if you have reservations or worries, respect their right to decide for themselves and to gain knowledge from their own experiences.

- **Act as a Friend and Mentor:** As your child grows older, the parent-child bond can transform into a friendship characterized by trust and respect for one another. When appropriate, impart wisdom and advice gleaned from your life experiences, but also be open to learning from your adult child's distinct viewpoints and experiences. Take advantage of the chance to develop and learn together.

- **Accept that Change is a Natural Component of Life and Relationships; Embrace it.** Accept the changing dynamics and be willing to modify your parental expectations and responsibilities. Stress the advantages of this transition, such as the chance to forge a more meaningful and lasting bond with your adult child.

- **Find Shared Interests:** Investigate and foster mutual pursuits that might deepen your relationship. Opportunities for connection and understanding can be created by participating in activities, attending events, or spending quality time together.

- **Let Go of Old Roles:** It can be difficult to let go of the dynamics and roles that were established throughout the development of your child. Give your adult child the freedom to define themselves independently of their past. Refrain from imposing your own standards on them and support them on their quest for self-discovery.

• **Handle Disagreements Maturely:** As you manage the shifting dynamics, conflicts may come up. Approach conflicts as they arise with maturity, respect, and an open mind. Instead of trying to establish who is right or wrong, concentrate on finding points of agreement and respecting one another's viewpoints.

• **Seek Professional Assistance if Necessary:** If you are having trouble adjusting to the new dynamics or if ongoing arguments are negatively affecting your relationship with your adult child, you might want to consider getting help from a family therapist or counselor. They can offer you direction and encouragement as you successfully negotiate this adjustment.

Always keep in mind that every parent-child connection is distinct, and adaptation calls for continual effort and comprehension on both sides. You can build an enduring and helpful relationship with your adult child by accepting the changing dynamics and encouraging a healthy and respectful connection.

## The potential conflicts that arise when parents struggle to let go and adult children seek independence

For both parents and their children, growing up is a time of significant change. Parents need to learn to relinquish control when their kids get older and leave the house. For some parents, who may find it challenging to accept their children's increased independence, this can be a challenging process.

Adult children are also fighting to make their own way in the world at the same time. They can be making fresh choices regarding their lifestyles, relationships, and employment. Children who are adults may find this to be a difficult period and require their parents' assistance as they adjust to these changes.

Conflict can result when parents find it difficult to let go and adult children want their independence. There are many ways in which this conflict can appear, including:

- **Disagreements Involving Money:** Even though their adult children are capable of supporting themselves, parents may feel compelled to give them financial help. Arguments over how much money should be donated, how it should be spent, and when it should stop can result from this.

- **Disagreements Over Dietary Habits:** Parents' expectations for their adult children's lifestyle decisions may differ from those of the children themselves. Arguments over everything from where to live to what to eat to how to spend leisure time might result from this.

- **Control Problems:** Some parents can find it difficult to relinquish influence over the life of their grown children. This may result in parents trying to micromanage their kids' behavior or micromanaging their decisions.

- **Different Morals:** Children may grow up with distinct values from their parents. Conflict over a variety of topics, including politics, religion, and how to raise their own children may result from this.

- **Not Enough Communication:** Misunderstandings are often the result of poor communication between parents and adult children. Even if the parents and adult children share identical ideals, a lack of clear communication can cause tension.

- **A Sense of Guilt:** Some parents can feel bad about parting with their kids. Even when it is not in the children's best interests, this guilt may cause them to strive to control their children's lives.

- **Emotions of Loss:** Parents could feel a sense of loss when their children leave the home. Conflict can occasionally result from management of this tough emotion.

The transition from childhood to adulthood is usually accompanied by conflict between parents and adult children. However, if conflict is not handled well, it can harm the bond between parents and children.

There are several things parents and adult children can do to lessen conflict and keep their relationship strong during this period, including:

• **Discuss Expectations:** Parents and adult children must discuss what they expect from one another. Expectations regarding money, way of life, and control are included. Parents and adult children can prevent misunderstandings and arguments by communicating about expectations.

• **Establish Limits:** Setting limits is crucial for both parents and adult children. This entails being considerate of one another's personal space and privacy. It entails refraining from attempting to influence one another's choices.

• **Be Encouraging:** Parents and adult children need to assist one another during this transition. This entails listening to one another, offering counsel when appropriate, and offering each other emotional support.

• **Assistance Should be Sought:** It may be beneficial to seek professional assistance if a conflict is seriously impacting the connection between the parents and their children. A therapist can support parents and adult children in improving communication and resolving conflict.

It's vital to keep in mind that you are not alone if you are having disagreements as parents with your adult children as they enter maturity. This is a typical occurrence, but there are steps you can take to minimize conflict and preserve your connection. You can ensure that this shift goes as smoothly as possible for everyone concerned by speaking clearly, establishing boundaries, and showing support.

# Chapter Two

## Understanding Boundaries and Autonomy

**Boundaries and Autonomy in the Context of Parent-child Relationships**

The dynamics of the parent-child connection naturally alter as children grow into adults. For both parents and their adult offspring, the change from being a dependent kid to an independent adult can occasionally be difficult. Setting up sound limits and encouraging autonomy are important aspects of navigating this change. While autonomy refers to the ability to make decisions and live one's life following chosen values and views, boundaries are the emotional and physical constraints that define an individual's personal space.

**Recognizing Boundaries**

Boundaries provide a foundation for individualism, self-care, and respect. Boundaries are crucial for both parties in the context of interactions between parents and adult children.

Parents should acknowledge and respect the boundaries set by their adult children so that they can create their own identities and make their own decisions. In addition, adult children should respect and clearly define their boundaries, encouraging candid communication in the relationship.

- **Emotional Boundaries:** Respecting one another's emotions, viewpoints, and privacy falls under the category of emotional boundaries. Parents should abstain from interfering too much or forcing their opinions on their grown offspring. Instead, they ought to make an effort to offer advice and support while making room for personal development. Conversely, adult children must communicate their feelings honestly and openly in order to create a culture of trust.

- **Physical Boundaries:** The right to privacy and personal space are both covered by physical boundaries. Parents need to understand that their adult children require autonomy and should respect their boundaries. It's important to refrain from being invasive and not searching through their possessions or accessing their personal space without permission. Adult children should respectfully express their need for privacy and personal space in return.

## Developing Autonomy

A vital component of personal development and growth is autonomy. Parents should encourage their adult children's quest for independence while also acting as a safety net and source of guidance when necessary. The following techniques can be used to promote autonomy in parent-adult-child relationships:

- **Encouragement of Decision-Making:** By encouraging their adult children to make decisions and accept responsibility for the results, parents can give their kids more independence. Instead of making decisions for adult children, parents should offer them support and direction so they can learn how to solve problems on their own.

- **Respecting Diverse Life Paths:** While parents may have expectations or objectives for their adult children, it's important to remember that every person has a different set of desires. Fostering autonomy and preserving a positive relationship depends on respecting and assisting their chosen routes, even if they diverge from the parents' vision.

- **Effective Communication:** This is essential to developing mutual respect and understanding between parents and their adult children. Open communication between the two parties is encouraged, along with honest listening without passing judgment. This strategy fosters a welcoming atmosphere where disputes can be discussed and amicably settled.

- **Allowing Mistakes:** Learning and development involves making mistakes. Even if it means that their decisions may result in failure or disappointment, parents should let their adult children make their own decisions and deal with the repercussions. Giving adult children a safety net and advice in trying times helps them become resilient and learn important life skills.

# The importance of establishing healthy boundaries for both parents and adult children

A delicate dance of independence and reliance unfolds as the relationship between parents and their children develops over time.

Healthy boundaries must be established as a result of the new dynamics and challenges that come with growing up. Setting boundaries is important for both parents and adult children because it promotes personal development, creates respect, upholds emotional stability, and fosters positive connections.

- **Encourage Personal Development:** Boundaries offer a crucial foundation for development and self-discovery. It encourages independence and a sense of autonomy when parents give their adult children the freedom to pursue their own values, beliefs, and interests. Similarly, adult children who set their own boundaries are free to explore who they are without feeling constrained by their parent's expectations. Healthy limits build a foundation for human progress by fostering individual development.

- **Respect:** Mutual respect between parents and adult children is built on a foundation of boundaries. It shows a deep regard for each other's individuality and autonomy when both parties are aware of and respect each other's boundaries.

Parents should acknowledge that their adult children can make decisions for themselves and should respect their boundaries. Adult children, on the other hand, should respect their parents' demand for autonomy, personal space, and privacy. Respectfully setting boundaries improves the quality of the relationship and encourages honest communication.

• **Keeping Your Emotional Health Alive:** Both parents and adult children need boundaries to maintain their emotional health. What is acceptable and what is not in terms of emotional support, communication, and involvement in each other's lives is determined by emotional boundaries.

Parents must understand that their adult children are in charge of their own emotions and shouldn't be subjected to undue emotional pressure. However, adult children must clearly express their emotional needs and limitations in order to avoid being overburdened by their parent's expectations. Both parties can safeguard their mental and emotional health and foster healthier relationships by upholding emotional boundaries.

# Common challenges faced by parents in setting boundaries and understanding their adult children's need for independence

Parenting is a lifelong endeavor involving many difficulties and changes. Parents frequently have to strike a fine balance as their children mature into adults by setting limits while acknowledging their need for freedom.

Both partners may have confusion and difficulty at this phase. The challenges parents frequently face when managing this dynamic will be covered here, along with practical methods for setting limits and encouraging a healthy feeling of independence for adult children.

• **Giving up the Parental Role**

Letting go of their long-held parental role is one of the biggest obstacles parents confront when trying to comprehend their adult children's need for independence. Making judgments and offering advice on behalf of their children is nothing new for parents. But as they grow older, their kids need the freedom to pursue their own interests, even if they don't align with those of their parents.

Parents frequently struggle with this transition because they are worried about their kids making errors or failing. They could also find it difficult to give up control and acknowledge that their kids can live independently. To get over this obstacle, parents must accept that their kids are now grownups, able to make thoughtful decisions, and gain knowledge from their experiences.

### • Communication Gap

Understanding the need for independence and boundaries of adult children depends heavily on effective communication; however, in this situation, communication failures can be a frequent problem. It can be challenging for parents to convey their worries or establish boundaries without coming across as tyrannical or intrusive, and adult children may find it difficult to express their need for independence without coming across as condescending or dismissive.

Parents should place a high priority on direct and honest communication to address this issue. They can get started by paying attention to their adult children's viewpoints, respecting their emotions, and gently expressing their own worries. Establishing a mutual understanding and respect for each other's needs can be achieved by having regular dialogues about expectations, boundaries, and goals.

### • Roles and Expectations Changing

Children's expectations and duties within the family dynamic alter significantly when they enter adulthood. Parents may have some preconceived assumptions about the future, career, or relationship choices of their adult offspring. In contrast, adult children may have distinct goals and aspirations from those of their parents.

Tension and conflict may result from this inconsistency in expectations and roles. Parents may find it difficult to accept the decisions made by their adult children and may unintentionally impose their own views. Parents must understand that their children are unique individuals with their own hopes and desires. Even if their adult children's journeys diverge from their own, they should encourage them to pursue their own goals.

### • Setting Good Boundaries

It's important to establish good boundaries in all relationships, especially those between parents and their adult children. Finding the ideal balance, though, can be difficult. Parents may find it challenging to distinguish between providing support and encouraging dependency. On the other hand, adult children could rebel against perceived limitations on their independence.

To overcome this obstacle, parents should set up clear, dependable boundaries while respecting the independence of their adult offspring. Expectations about duties, financial assistance, and decision-making procedures must be clearly communicated.

# Chapter Three

## Effective Communication Strategies

### The Significance of Open and Honest Communication in Bridging the Generational Gap

In today's culture, we frequently find ourselves coexisting alongside generations, each with its own distinct set of values, life experiences, and communication preferences. These generational distinctions can occasionally cause miscommunications, disputes, and a worsening of the generational gap. Honest and open dialogue can help close these gaps and promote respect and peace among generations.

### Getting to Know the Generational Gap

The difference in attitudes, beliefs, and behaviors between generations is referred to as the generational gap. Different historical, cultural, and technical circumstances that have shaped each generation's experiences and viewpoints are the cause of these variations.

The Silent Generation, Baby Boomers, Generation X, Millennials, and Generation Z are some of the major generations alive today. Each of these generations experienced different social upheavals, technical developments, and cultural transitions throughout their formative years.

### Problems Resulting from the Generational Gap

The age divide can provide some difficulties, such as misunderstandings, preconceptions, and a lack of empathy. Each generation favors different communication styles and tactics.

For instance, whereas younger generations frequently favor digital communication channels like social media, messaging apps, and email, older generations may rely more on in-person contacts, phone conversations, or more formally written correspondence. These divergent communication styles can cause miscommunications and obstruct productive conversation.

The generational divide can also be exacerbated by prejudices and preconceived assumptions about certain generations. For example, older generations may consider younger generations as entitled, slothful, or lacking in work ethic, while new generations may see older generations as resistant to change, technologically illiterate, or out of touch with contemporary trends. These misconceptions can obstruct honest and free conversation and impede lasting ties between generations.

## The benefits of honest and open communication

An effective approach for bridging the generational divide is open and honest communication. Sincere conversations between people of different generations can help them understand one another's viewpoints, experiences, and values. It promotes empathy, eliminates stereotypes, and fosters an atmosphere of respect and understanding.

- **Listening and Understanding**

Active listening and a sincere effort to comprehend the other person's viewpoint are the foundations of effective communication. Every generation contributes distinctive wisdom based on their experiences. We can find common ground and identify the principles that cut across generational lines by carefully listening and trying to understand. This strategy promotes intergenerational cooperation and creates respect for one another.

- **Communication Styles Adaptation**

It is crucial to modify communication strategies to match the demands of various generations if we are to close the generational divide.

While younger generations are at ease using digital communication platforms, older generations may prefer in-person or phone talks. People can interact with others across generations more successfully by striking a balance and employing a variety of communication techniques.

### • Accepting Technological Developments

The way we interact has been dramatically impacted by technological improvements. By assisting older generations in adjusting to new communication tools, younger generations who have grown up surrounded by technology, can be crucial in closing the generational divide.

Digital platforms, social media, and online resources can provide new opportunities for communication and comprehension if you gently guide them through them.

### • Sharing Wisdom and Knowledge

Every age has its own distinct body of knowledge and wisdom. Younger generations contribute new perspectives and creative ideas, while older generations have a wealth of knowledge and life lessons to impart.

These ideas can only be shared by open and honest dialogue, which helps both parties develop. Sharing information across generations fosters a sense of community and promotes lifelong learning.

### • Creating Solid Relationships

Strong relationships between generations can only be established based on open and honest conversation. Open communication between people fosters an environment of transparency, sincerity, and trust.

This makes it possible for them to resolve disputes, misunderstandings, and differences amicably. Generational prejudices can be overcome and people can gain a better understanding and respect for one another by having an open discourse.

### • Opportunities for Mentoring and Education

Mentoring and educational possibilities are made possible through effective generational communication. Older generations can mentor younger generations by imparting their experience and wisdom. This mentoring relationship may offer priceless advice for developing personally and professionally. For example, parents can teach their children how to file income taxes, questions to ask when purchasing auto or health insurance, or what to look for when buying a car or house.

Younger generations can simultaneously introduce older ones to cutting-edge technologies, social movements, and novel concepts, promoting lifelong learning and development. For example, children can teach their parents about new social media or money transfer apps, how to safely buy items online without getting scammed, or help them learn about online services for construction projects and even online mobile car detailing.

### • Fostering Creativity and Innovation

By fusing many viewpoints and ideas, open and honest communication fosters innovation and creativity.

Drawing from their distinct experiences, each generation approaches problem-solving and decision-making differently.

Generations can work together to create creative solutions and promote change by promoting open communication and providing a safe environment for exchanging ideas.

### • Building a Peaceful Society

A peaceful and cohesive society is largely the result of open and honest communication. To address societal issues, advance social advancement, and create a sustainable future, generations must collaborate. People can develop a sense of togetherness and common purpose through meaningful interactions that provide insights into the needs, goals, and concerns of many generations.

**Effective Generational Communication Tips**

• Show genuine interest in the opinions and experiences of others by practicing active listening. When you need more information, ask for it while paying close attention.

• Be receptive to different points of view and willing to question your own biases and preconceptions. Parents and their adult children must be open-minded when discussing various topics. In today's society, people are dealing with all types of issues, and the older generation may be struggling with how to relate to the younger generation in terms of communication.

• Consider changing the way you communicate: various generations may like to communicate in different ways. Be willing to change your approach to suit other people's demands and be adaptable in the way you communicate.

• Encourage empathy and understanding by putting yourself in other people's shoes and making an effort to comprehend their distinctive viewpoints and experiences. This will aid in bridging the empathy gap.

• Promote intergenerational cooperation by giving different generations the chance to cooperate, share ideas, and gain from one another.

• Be respectful and considerate: Regardless of differences in beliefs or ideals, show kindness and respect to people of all ages.

• Accept lifelong learning: See every interaction as a chance to improve and learn. Recognize that people of all ages can teach you things

# Practical tips for active listening and effective expression of thoughts and emotions

Healthy and happy relationships depend heavily on communication, particularly between parents and their adult children. However, generational differences, varying perspectives, and emotional dynamics can occasionally make it difficult to communicate effectively. In order to close these gaps and promote understanding and connection, active listening and the effective expression of thoughts and feelings are essential.

- **Develop Empathy:** Effective communication is built on empathy. Adult children and their parents should make an effort to comprehend and value one another's viewpoints, feelings, and experiences. Suspending judgment and actively listening is necessary for empathy. Consider the other person's perspective and make a sincere effort to comprehend it. The basis for honest and open communication is laid by this procedure.

- **Practice Active Listening:** Meaningful communication is made possible by the effective use of active listening. It entails paying full attention, maintaining eye contact, and appropriately responding. Set aside your distractions and pay close attention to what your adult child or parent is saying when you are speaking with them. It's best to refrain from speaking out while they're talking or preparing your response. Instead, give them space to completely express themselves before offering your opinions.

- **Validate Emotions:** Emotions are an essential component of communication, thus it's important to validate them. The feelings of parents and adult children should both be acknowledged and supported.

Recognizing and respecting the other person's emotional experience is what it means to validate another person's emotions rather than necessarily agreeing with them. For instance, you might respond to your adult child's irritation by saying, "I understand that you're feeling frustrated, and I'm here to listen." Providing emotional support encourages openness and trust.

• **Use "I" Statements:** Effective presentation of ideas and feelings demands boldness and clarity. Use "I" words to convey your sentiments and needs rather than accusing or blaming language. Saying "You never listen to me," for example, it is preferable to say "I feel unheard when I share my thoughts, and I would appreciate it if we could have a more open conversation." "I" statements present your point of view without placing blame, reducing defensiveness, and promoting fruitful discussion.

• **Practice Non-Defensive Communication:** It's typical for both parents and adult children to feel defensive during conversations, particularly when broaching delicate subjects.

Defensiveness prevents clear communication and frequently results in misunderstandings and disputes. Instead, make an effort to communicate without becoming defensive. This entails hearing the other person out without interrupting, accepting their point of view, and responding in a cool, courteous manner. You foster an environment that is receptive to understanding and compromise by remaining objective and non-defensive.

• **Prioritize Seeking Mutual Understanding:** Make this your top priority instead of just concentrating on making your case. Spend some time learning about and comprehending one another's viewpoints, values, and needs. Active listening, empathy, and a sincere desire to connect on a deeper level are necessary for this process.

Engage in meaningful conversations and open-ended inquiries to encourage both sides to express their thoughts and feelings. Mutual understanding helps to solve issues effectively and improves the relationship between parents and adult children.

- **Practice Mindful Communication:** Promoting mindful communication between parents and adult children helps improve communication and foster a better understanding between them. Being fully present in the conversation, paying attention to your own thoughts and feelings, and purposefully selecting your words and actions are all aspects of mindful communication. Here are some suggestions for how to communicate more mindfully:

a. **Take a Moment to Pause and Reflect:** Before responding to a comment or inquiry, pause and consider your response. This enables you to collect your thoughts so that you may answer thoughtfully and carefully as opposed to behaving quickly. Pauses taken intentionally serve to clear up confusion and advance effective communication.

b. **Pay Attention to Body Language:** Be aware of both your own and the other person's body language. Important signals can be conveyed through nonverbal cues. Are you displaying a defensive posture by crossing your arms or leaning away? Does the other individual seem uncomfortable or frustrated? Being aware of body language can assist you in responding empathetically and understanding the underlying feelings.

c. **Take Deep Breaths:** Controlling your emotions and clearing your mind are both possible with the help of deep breathing. Take a few deep breaths to relax if you see your anxiety levels increasing throughout a chat. This encourages improved communication by assisting you in approaching the topic with a more composed and relaxed attitude.

d. **Be Present:** It is simple to allow your thoughts to wander or become preoccupied with formulating your reply as the other person speaks. But mindful speaking necessitates staying completely in the present. By concentrating on the speaker's words, tone, and emotions, practice active listening. This demonstrates respect and improves your comprehension of their viewpoint.

- **Practice Not Passing Judgment:** Mindful communication is putting one's own opinions aside and entering a dialogue with an open mind. Never assume the motives or motivations of another person or jump to conclusions about them. Instead, listen with inquiry and sincere attention in order to comprehend their perspective free of prejudice.

● **Foster a Safe and Supportive Atmosphere:** Open and honest communication between parents and adult children requires a safe and supportive atmosphere. Make sure that neither party feels uncomfortable discussing their ideas or feelings without worrying about being judged or criticized.

Encourage an environment of trust and acceptance where people are valued and respected for their sentiments. The relationship between parents and adult children is strengthened when both parties engage in open communication and are receptive to criticism.

# The importance of empathy and understanding when engaging in conversations with adult children

As parents, we continue to play an important part in our kids' lives as they become older. Developing positive and meaningful relationships with our adult children becomes even more crucial.

The use of empathy and understanding in our talks is one of the crucial components that can greatly improve these relationships. We can foster an atmosphere of open communication, trust, and respect that promotes development and support for one another by fostering these traits.

### Recognizing Each Person's Unique Experiences

Empathy is the capacity to comprehend and experience another person's emotions. It is important to remember that our adult children have their own distinct experiences, viewpoints, and emotions while speaking with them. It's crucial to put aside any assumptions or preconceived notions that we as parents may have about their lives and enter dialogues with an open mind. By respecting their uniqueness, we give them the freedom to express themselves in their truest form, which builds trust and emotional ties.

Active listening is an essential element of successful communication. It entails paying attention to non-verbal signs, emotions, and underlying meanings in addition to hearing the stated words.

Being present and paying attention to what our adult children have to say during talks is crucial. This entails setting aside interruptions and giving them our whole focus. We can deepen our relationship with others by showing them that we value their opinions and feelings by carefully listening to them.

### Validating Their Feelings

Developing empathy requires an understanding of the feelings our adult children go through. Recognizing and accepting their emotions entails validating them, even if we don't quite concur with or understand them.

By doing this, we give children a place where they may express themselves without worrying about being judged or criticized. An increased level of emotional closeness and a stronger link between parent and kid are made possible by this validation, which gives them the understanding and support they need.

### Avoiding Assumptions and Judgment

Empathy calls on us to abstain from assuming anything about our adult offspring or casting judgment on them. Although our experiences and beliefs can influence our viewpoints, it is important to keep in mind that each person's perspective has a different history. We should approach interactions with interest and a desire to comprehend the other person's viewpoint. This way of thinking enriches the relationship between parents and adult children, facilitates a positive interchange of ideas, and supports each person's personal development.

### Help and Advice

Although it's crucial to respect our adult children's autonomy, they nevertheless need our help and advice. However, it could be necessary to alter the strategy from when they were younger.

Empathy enables us to be supportive by actively listening, posing open-ended questions, and providing aid when required, as opposed to offering unsolicited advice or exerting control. This method encourages a connection based on trust and understanding by giving our adult children the freedom to make their own decisions while being assured of our constant support.

Embracing Vulnerability: In order to connect with our adult children on a genuine level, we must be prepared to accept our own vulnerability. Sharing our views, experiences, and feelings with our adult children helps foster a greater sense of empathy and understanding.

By being open and vulnerable with others, we show them that we respect and trust them and encourage a mutually respectful dialogue in which both parties are free to voice their viewpoints. We create an example for our adult children to follow by being open and vulnerable, which ultimately strengthens our relationship.

## Developing Patience and Empathetic Communication

Empathy demands understanding and patience, particularly during difficult conversations or when disputes erupt.

It's critical to address these circumstances with composure and empathy, trying to understand before trying to be understood. We may cultivate an environment where open communication can flourish by paying attention carefully, refraining from interjecting and speaking in a non-confrontational manner. We can negotiate through differences with patience, identify common ground, and come to agreements that respect both sides' viewpoints.

## Celebrating Their Successes and Development

As parents, it is crucial to acknowledge our adult children's successes and development.

When parents show their children true pride, joy, and encouragement for their accomplishments, it not only deepens the parent-child relationship but also gives them a sense of self-worth. By praising their achievements, large or small, we validate their efforts and acknowledge their skills, fostering a good and encouraging relationship.

## The Learning Process

Empathy and understanding are abilities that need constant development. It's critical to understand that learning from our mistakes and progressing are necessary parts of the journey. We may continually hone our communication abilities and broaden our comprehension of our adult children's needs and viewpoints by reflecting on ourselves and being open to their input. We can strengthen our bonds with our adult children and maintain our loving and supportive relationship by remaining flexible and open to change.

# Chapter Four

## Letting Go of Control

**The Fear and Emotional Challenges Parents May Experience when Relinquishing Control**

Parenting is a never-ending journey full of joy, love, and difficulties. Parents intuitively assume the roles of protector and provider the moment their child is born. They assist, counsel, and reassure their kids as they navigate different phases of life. But as kids develop into adults, a natural shift takes place in which parents must learn to relinquish control and let their kids discover the world on their own. As they struggle with the realization that their children are no longer dependent on them, many parents may experience dread and emotional difficulties throughout this transition.

The strong emotional connection parents form with their children is what causes the anxiety of letting go. They have invested countless hours in the upbringing of their children over the years.

Parents may be concerned about their children's capacity to make moral decisions, navigate obstacles, and ultimately thrive in life as they grow up. This anxiety is frequently driven by parents' worry about their children's future and their desire to shield them from harm.

A sense of loss is one of the major emotional obstacles' parents encounter when giving up control. Parents who relinquish the role they have played for so long may experience a hole in their lives. As their children grow more autonomous, the daily interactions, the sense of fulfillment they gain from parenting, and the intimacy they once shared with them may wane. Parents who have built their lives on their children may experience sadness, emptiness, and even an identity crisis as a result of this loss.

The anxiety of making mistakes is another emotional obstacle. Parents frequently feel a great deal of responsibility for the success and welfare of their kids. They may wonder about their former parenting choices and worry about the ramifications when they stand back and let their adult offspring take the helm.

They can worry that they haven't given their kids the best chance to succeed or that they have unintentionally stifled their development as adults. Parents may find it difficult to let go and have faith in their children's skills because of this paralyzing fear.

Additionally, the inability of parents to give up control might be impacted by the fear of criticism. Society frequently lays demands on parents, holding them responsible for the accomplishments and behavior of their kids.

The fear of being perceived as a failure or inept can motivate parents to maintain control over the lives of their adult children. Parents may find it difficult to give their kids the freedom to make their own decisions and discover their own mistakes due to the need to uphold the image of good parenting.

Parents must understand the value of letting go in order to handle these anxieties and emotional difficulties. It is essential for the growth and development of both parties and a natural component of the parent-child interaction. Parents can use the following techniques to make the process easier:

- **Develop Trust:** It's crucial to lay a foundation of trust between parents and adult children. Parents must have confidence in their kids' capacity to make wise decisions and navigate the obstacles of life. As parents share their worries and expectations while giving their kids the freedom to express their own ideas and thoughts, open and honest communication can help build trust.

- **Practice Self-Care:** Self-care is important because giving up control can be emotionally taxing. Parents must put their own needs first while also figuring out how to fill the hole created by their children's independence.

Parents can maintain a sense of purpose and fulfillment outside of their parental role by partaking in self-care activities such as hobbies, exercise, socializing with friends, or pursuing personal interests. Parents will gain by looking after their own physical, emotional, and mental health since it will let them support their adult children more skillfully.

• **Seek Assistance:** Parents may find it helpful to seek assistance from those who have or are undergoing similar experiences. Joining support groups, going to counseling, or getting therapy can give parents a secure place to voice their worries, uncertainties, and feelings. Sharing experiences and picking up tips from others can provide insightful guidance and coping mechanisms to help people move through the transition of letting go.

• **Adopt a Growth Mindset:** Adopting a growth mindset allows parents to recognize their own and their adult children's capacity for personal development. The anxiety of making mistakes might be reduced by realizing that learning from mistakes and developing personally come from experience. Resilience and independence can be fostered by parents encouraging their adult children to take chances, learn from mistakes, and seize new possibilities.

• **Focus on the Now:** Parents must embrace the present moment rather than getting caught up in the past or the future. Accepting that their adult children are on their own paths and can make their own decisions demands letting go of control.

In their relationships with their children, parents can cultivate mindfulness and practice being totally present, savoring the intimate moments, and encouraging their independence.

• **Celebrate Achievements:** Instead of concentrating only on the difficulties and worries related to letting go, parents should take the time to recognize and honor the accomplishments of their adult children.

Recognizing their accomplishments, no matter how big or tiny, can boost parents' faith in their kids' skills and reassure them that they are headed in the right direction. A spirit of respect and admiration for one another can be fostered by sharing a celebration with parents and adult children.

The process of relinquishing control takes time, introspection, and flexibility. Parents must keep in mind that when their children mature into adults, their role as mentors and supporters changes.

Parents can build a healthier, more harmonious connection with their adult children by accepting the required changes and confronting their anxieties head-on.

In the end, relinquishing control enables both parents and adult children to experience personal development, independence, and the satisfaction that comes from handling life's obstacles alone.

## Guidance on how to gradually release control and allow adult children to make their own decisions

One of our priorities as parents is to create independent, self-reliant children who are capable of navigating the challenges of adult life.

Although it can be difficult to let go and let our kids make their own decisions, it is necessary. Giving children the opportunity to choose their own paths while also providing them with direction demands a careful balance.

### Understand the Value of Independence

Recognizing how important it is for our children to develop independence in their life is the first step in relinquishing control as a parent. Independence enables individuals to acquire vital life skills, boost their self-esteem, and gain knowledge from their own experiences. It is vital to know that our job shifts from being the main decision-maker to that of a trusted advisor and supporter. Accepting this change empowers our adult children to accept responsibility for their decisions and promotes personal development.

## Promote Candid Communication

Any healthy relationship, including the parent-child bond, is built on effective communication. It's crucial to develop direct lines of communication with your teen age children in order to gradually relinquish power. Encourage them to communicate their ideas, worries, and desires openly and without inhibition.

Even if you don't share their opinions, pay attention and support their sentiments. You can learn important information about their decision-making processes and, if required, offer direction by encouraging open communication.

## Promoting Self-Analysis and Self-Awareness

For decision-making and personal development, self-reflection and self-awareness are essential skills. Asking themselves questions such as, "What do I truly want?" or "What are my values and beliefs?" is something you should encourage your teen age children to do.

Encourage them to recognize that the process of self-discovery is a lifelong one and that it's acceptable to make mistakes along the way. By encouraging self-awareness, you enable people to make decisions that are in line with their own values rather than relying exclusively on external validation or acceptance.

# Progressive independence with growing responsibilities

Giving your teen age children more and more responsibility and chances to make decisions will help you gradually relinquish control. Start by assigning simple duties or errands so they can gain confidence in their skills. Allow them to handle tasks like planning their calendars, managing their accounts, or preparing meals, for instance. Expand their duties as they prove themselves capable, providing them more freedom to make significant life decisions.

Giving your adult children supportive guidance entails mentoring, using positive reinforcement, and when asked, imparting your expertise. It does not imply telling them what to do. Be a sounding board for them and encourage them to talk to you about their thoughts and worries.

Share your personal experiences and provide advice, but keep in mind that your decisions may not have been the same as theirs. Believe in their ability and respect their judgment. They will feel empowered as a result of this support, which will inspire them to take responsibility for their choices.

**Accept Mistakes and Their Individuality**

Every person is different, with their own interests, goals, and morals. As parents, we must value and celebrate each child's uniqueness. Don't impose your own objectives or expectations on others. Even if their decisions diverge from what you had in mind for them, allow them to consider several options. Recognize that making mistakes is a necessary part of learning, and try not to be too harsh or judgmental. Instead, create a safe space where they may openly share their experiences and learn from their failures.

# The benefits of fostering independence and self-reliance in adult children

One of our main objectives as parents is to bring up our kids to be capable, self-assured, and independent individuals. Our children's long-term success and personal development depend on us to help them develop independence and self-reliance. By helping children to grow in these areas, we equip them with the tools they need to face obstacles in life, make moral choices, and prosper in a dynamic environment. We shall examine the many advantages of encouraging adult children's independence and self-reliance here.

- **Improved Problem-Solving Skills:** By encouraging our kids' independence, we provide them with the critical problem-solving abilities they need. Children learn to evaluate situations, think critically, and come up with original solutions when they are allowed the opportunity to make decisions and deal with issues on their own. This will help them face obstacles with confidence throughout their life.

- **Enhanced Self-Confidence:** Self-confidence is enhanced by independence and self-reliance. Children gain a sense of competence and self-belief when they are encouraged to take responsibility for their actions and make decisions on their own.

They can approach new situations and take on problems since they are confident and don't worry about failing. By encouraging independence, parents help their kids develop self-esteem, which is essential for their general success and well-being.

- **Increased Resilience:** Because life is full of ups and downs, resilience is an essential quality to possess when navigating its difficulties. Giving kids the flexibility to solve problems on their own teaches them how to adjust, endure, and overcome obstacles.

Parents that encourage independence in their children are teaching them that obstacles are a part of life and that they have the fortitude and tenacity to overcome them. Their ability to manage difficulties with poise and tenacity thanks to this resilience will benefit them both personally and professionally.

- **Improved Decision-Making Capabilities:** Children who are independent and self-reliant can make good decisions. Children gain decision-making abilities and learn to trust their judgment when given the chance to make decisions and take responsibility for the results.

This capacity to make wise decisions becomes more crucial as kids mature into adults. By encouraging independence, parents provide their kids the chance to practice making decisions in a safe setting, which will help them later in life when they have more responsibility.

- **Improved Time Management:** Children who are independent and self-reliant are more likely to take control of their time and learn efficient time management techniques. Children learn the value of time and how to prioritize chores when they are free to plan and organize their calendars. For example, parents can set up a chore and homework calendar for kids to learn how to manage their time when they are young. This pairs well with a positive reinforcement reward system.

As kids enter adulthood, where juggling various commitments and duties becomes the norm, this skill becomes more and more important. By encouraging independence, parents provide their kids with the tools they need to manage their time effectively, which boosts their output and overall success. Adult children will be able to implement their own form of time management because their parents took the time to teach them years ago.

• **Increased Accountability:** Encouraging children's independence also instills in them a sense of responsibility. They learn the value of being accountable for the results that follow when they are encouraged to take ownership of their choices and actions.

Children who are held accountable for their actions grow in honesty, dependability, and a solid work ethic. These traits become more important as children grow into adults because they help people establish trust in their personal and professional relationships and succeed in a variety of endeavors. For example, let's say your child is taking an AP college class in high school and they forget to study for a test, so they decide to cheat. The teacher catches them cheating and due to school's integrity policy, they get kicked out of the class. As parents, we want to protect our child from this; however, this is a valuable life lesson and they should be held accountable for their actions.

• **Improved Emotional Well-Being:** Adult children's emotional well-being is influenced by their independence and self-reliance. Children are more likely to have a strong sense of identity and purpose when they are encouraged to develop independence.

They grow less dependent on other people for approval, which lessens the chance that they would form unhealthy dependencies or depend on other people or things to make them happy. Fostering independence enables kids to form a positive sense of self, which enhances their emotional resiliency and general well-being.

• **Improved Life Skills:** Adult children who are encouraged to be independent and self-reliant gain vital life skills that are required for a successful and meaningful life.

When young people are encouraged to take on duties like running a household, handling money, cooking, cleaning, and preserving relationships, they develop practical skills that are essential for daily life. They are equipped with these skills to take care of themselves, as well as to positively impact their communities and develop into well-rounded people.

• **Empowered Personal Growth:** By encouraging independence, parents provide their adult children a platform to set out on a path of personal development and self-discovery. People experience a high sense of personal agency and fulfillment when they are allowed the freedom to pursue their goals, make decisions that are consistent with their values, and explore their interests. Fostering independence enables adult children to identify their interests, skills, and special abilities, which eventually results in a more fulfilling and purposeful life.

• **Stronger Parent-Child Relationship:** It's ironic, but encouraging adult children's independence and self-reliance can really make parents and kids closer. Children become less dependent on their parents for ongoing assistance and direction as they grow more independent.

However, this change in the dynamics of the relationship may result in a closer connection based on respect and understanding for one another. Parents can develop into dependable mentors and friends in addition to being supportive. Parents build a connection built on trust and open communication with their adult children by giving them the freedom to make their own decisions.

Parenting's ultimate purpose is to prepare kids for life, where they will encounter a variety of obligations and difficulties. Children who are encouraged to be independent and self-reliant from an early age will be better prepared to meet the rigors of adulthood with maturity. Parents facilitate a smooth transition into the real world so that adult children may confidently navigate their employment, relationships, and personal lives by gradually delegating responsibilities and fostering independence.

# Chapter Five

## Adjusting Expectations

**Common Unrealistic Expectations Parents May Have of their Adult Children**

The dynamics between parents and their children always change as children grow into adults since parenting is a lifelong journey. However, parents sometimes find it difficult to modify their expectations in accordance with reality because they cling to unrealistic ideals of what their adult children should be. Although it is common for parents to have hopes and ambitions for the future of their children, it is crucial to understand that having unreasonable expectations can harm relationships and impede personal development.

In this part, we'll examine some typical, unrealistic expectations that parents may have for their adult children and clarify what growing up really entails.

**Job Choices**

Concerning the job choices of their adult children, parents frequently have unreasonable expectations. Parents frequently aspire for their children to pursue particular careers or follow in their footsteps.

While mentoring and encouragement are critical, it's important to keep in mind that every person has unique passions, talents, and aspirations. Pressuring adult children to achieve their parents' professional goals might cause bitterness and a lack of self-worth. Giving adult children the freedom to explore and make their own decisions while accepting their individual success path is crucial.

**Relationships and Marriage**

Parents may have preconceived beliefs about the love life of their adult children, anticipating that they will settle down, get married, or have children by a particular age. These demands may place adult children under excessive pressure, resulting in interpersonal tension and strain.

It is critical to keep in mind that each person's path through love is unique, and rushing or imposing timeframes might have negative consequences. Stronger friendships and open communication result from supporting adult children in their quest for happy relationships, regardless of cultural conventions or expectations.

## Financial Independence

Financial Independence is another area where irrational expectations frequently surface. Parents may have a target date in mind for their adult offspring to achieve a certain level of accomplishment or financial stability. The economic picture of today is, however, very different from that of earlier generations.

The difficulty of gaining financial independence is increased by factors such as the lack of employment opportunities, growing living expenses, and student loan debt. Instead of imposing unreasonable deadlines or placing excessive stress on financial problems, parents must acknowledge these difficulties and provide support and counsel.

## Parental Control and Decision-Making

Even in situations where autonomy is expected, parents who find it difficult to relinquish control may continue to exercise influence over their adult children's choices. This might involve interfering with important life decisions or micromanaging individual choices. Allowing adult children the freedom to make their own decisions is essential for personal growth and the development of self-confidence, even though parents may have their children's best interests at heart. Adult children can learn from their experiences and forge a strong sense of identity when their autonomy is supported.

Parents may have high expectations for their adult offspring to reach particular milestones or achieve perfection in a variety of spheres of life. As people struggle to meet expectations that do not align with their own goals, this pressure can cause feelings of inadequacy and worry.

It is essential to acknowledge that each person has a distinct journey and meaning of success. A caring environment that promotes resilience and happiness can be created by encouraging personal development, self-compassion, and applauding individual accomplishments, no matter how minor.

# Reassessing parent's expectations and embracing the reality of their children's lives

Let's discuss the need of reevaluating parental expectations and respecting the unique journeys our adult children take.

**Understanding the Shift**

As kids grow into adults, their interests, goals, and aspirations change. The reality is that their children are now capable individuals who can make their own decisions and this transition must be acknowledged by parents. By changing expectations, parents can promote a culture that values direct communication, respect for individuality, and understanding.

Parents typically have an idealized vision for how their children's lives should pan out. However, it's crucial to give up control and permit your grown children to make their own decisions. Even while it may be upsetting to see our kids select their own paths, it's crucial to trust in their abilities and respect their choices, even if they don't line up with our own expectations for them.

Healthy communication is the cornerstone of any relationship, including that between parents and adult children. By promoting honest and open conversation, parents can discover more about their children's aspirations, challenges, and goals. Through this perspective exchange, parents can better support their adult children by comprehending their motivations and providing them with the support they need.

Parents usually have definite expectations for their children's personal relationships, academic performance, and career paths. However, as a result of these expectations, both partners could experience unjustified pressure and tension. We allow our older children the flexibility to explore their own passions and find their own sense of fulfillment by reassessing and changing our expectations. Instead of encouraging children to fixate on preconceived notions, we should help them discover their passions and develop their own sense of purpose.

Each person has particular skills, constraints, and objectives. Accepting the truth of our adult children's existence is necessary to appreciate their uniqueness. By respecting and supporting their unique qualities, parents can aid in their children's development of independence and self-confidence.

Although worrying about the welfare of our adult children is normal, it is crucial to give help without any terms or constraints. By always being there for them, we provide a safe space where children can turn for guidance, advice, and comfort. It encourages the belief that even if their efforts fall short of our expectations, we should still support them regardless of how they turn out.

# Chapter Six

## Balancing Support and Empowerment

**The Delicate Balance Between Offering Support and Empowering Adult Children**

The dynamics of the parent-child connection change as children mature into adults, and parenting is a lifelong journey. Finding the fine balance between providing support and giving their adult children autonomy is one of the difficulties parents encounter throughout this transition. It's normal for parents to want to protect and discipline their kids, but it's also crucial to encourage independence and self-sufficiency. To strike this equilibrium, one must be willing to adjust to shifting positions, have open communication, and respect one another.

As kids grow older, they start to make their own choices, deal with their own difficulties, and gain knowledge through their own mistakes. Their personal development and growth are absolutely necessary during this time of transition. In order to provide their adult children the freedom to take charge of their life and learn from both achievements and disappointments, parents must acknowledge and support their autonomy.

Offering assistance does not imply total abandonment, though. Parents still have a responsibility to act as a safety net for their grown children. This may entail providing counsel, listening, and emotional support as needed. Striking a balance between being accessible and involved without becoming overbearing or dominating is crucial.

An essential component of keeping this equilibrium is effective communication. To encourage their adult children to voice their ideas, worries, and aspirations, parents should create a safe and open environment.

It is essential to attentively listen, without passing judgment, and to validate their feelings. Parents can then comprehend their adult children's needs and offer support in a meaningful and helpful way.

Encouragement to form their own identities, make choices, and accept responsibility are all aspects of empowering adult children. Particularly for parents who are accustomed to being actively involved in their children's lives, this can be a difficult process. Allowing adult children to make their own decisions, even if they go against their parents' desires, is crucial for their development as individuals and for helping them find who they are.

Allowing grown children to learn from their mistakes is another aspect of empowerment. Even though it can be painful to watch them fall, it's important to fight the impulse to help them out of every jam.

Adversity and failure can teach us important lessons about resilience and problem-solving techniques. Parents can help adult children grow their own coping skills and self-confidence by stepping back and letting them handle issues on their own.

It is crucial to understand that the ratio of support to empowerment can change based on the person and the particular situation. While some adult children might need more direction and support, others might be more autonomous and self-sufficient. Parents should be aware of the particular needs of their children and offer the right amount of support for those needs.

Finally, achieving the right balance between supporting and empowering adult children involves flexibility, effective communication, and respect for their autonomy. Parents must understand how crucial it is to let their adult children make their own decisions, overcome obstacles, and gain wisdom from their experiences.

Parents may equip their children to traverse the challenges of adulthood while knowing they have a loving and caring foundation to fall back on by encouraging independence and self-sufficiency in them.

## Strategies for providing guidance without being

# controlling or overbearing

The process of raising children continues long after they become adults since it is a lifelong endeavor. Although it can be challenging to strike the right balance between being supportive and controlling, as parents, we want to continue to provide our adult children with guidance and support. Here are some methods for guiding grown children without being pushy or controlling:

- **Become a Listening Ear:** Being a sounding board for adult children is one of the best ways to provide direction to them. Allow them to talk to you about their issues and difficulties while providing a listening ear and support. Instead of attempting to fix their problems for them, just listen and, if requested, offer suggestions.

- **Instead of Lecturing, Pose Questions:** Instead of lecturing your adult child when they seek advice, engage them in conversation. They can use this to think through their issues and develop original answers. Additionally, it will demonstrate your appreciation for their autonomy to them.

- **Be Encouraging Rather than Critical:** Be encouraging and understanding when your adult child errs. Avoid criticizing them or telling them they acted improperly. Instead, provide a hand and assist them in making amends for their errors.

- **Your Life is Your Own:** It's crucial to live your own life and avoid getting too involved in that of your adult child. This entails engaging in your own interests and hobbies, hanging out with your own friends and family, and working towards your own objectives. It also entails avoiding becoming your adult child's sole source of support.

- **Be Tolerant:** It takes time for adult children to develop the ability to make independent choices and lead independent lives. Don't be impatient with them and don't anticipate them to always make the right decisions.

• **Be Considerate:** Your adult child deserves your respect even though they are an adult now. Even if you disagree with their beliefs, show them respect and consider what they have to say.

• **Be Available:** Be there for your adult child when they need you. Offer them your assistance and support as they navigate their difficulties.

# Chapter Seven

## Strengthening the Parent-Child Bond

**Practical Tools and Exercises to Strengthen the Bond Between Parents and Adult Children**

For parents, keeping a close relationship with their adult children can be gratifying and meaningful. Parents must modify their approach as their children grow into adults since their demands and dynamics alter. It takes open communication, mutual respect, and shared experiences to create a solid friendship. In this section, we'll look at some useful techniques and activities that parents may use to develop love, understanding, and support with their adult children.

- **Active Listening:** The basis of any wholesome relationship is effective communication. A strong communication skill that helps strengthen the bond between parents and their adult children is active listening.

It entails paying full attention, maintaining eye contact, and sincerely hearing what the other person has to say without interjecting or drawing conclusions before they've finished. By showing empathy and confirming your adult child's feelings, even if you don't agree with them, you are engaging in active listening. This promotes open communication and trust.

- **Regular Check-Ins:** As children become older and move away, it can be easy to lose touch with loved ones due to life's busyness. A strong friendship can be maintained by establishing a habit of checking in on each other.

A weekly phone conversation, online chat, or in-person meeting should be set aside for catching up and exchanging life updates. The regularity of these check-ins reinforces your bond with your adult child and demonstrates to them that they are a priority.

• **Shared Activities:** Participating in shared activities can enhance the link between parents and adult children and help to develop lifelong memories. Discover shared hobbies and make plans for activities you can do together, such as making a meal, going on hikes, going to concerts, or even enrolling in a class. These shared activities encourage a sense of community and present an opportunity for in-depth discussions and quality time.

• **Practice Non-Judgment:** As our children grow older, it can be difficult for parents to relinquish their parental guidance and protectorship. It's critical to recognize that kids can now make independent decisions and choices.

Allowing others to voice their thoughts, make mistakes, and gain from their experiences is a key component of non-judgment. When asked, provide assistance and direction, but refrain from imposing your personal opinions. Your adult child will feel respected and cherished as a result, which promotes open communication.

• **Family Rituals and Traditions:** Having a sense of continuity and belonging is made possible by family rituals and customs. Create or uphold significant rituals that your adult children can participate in. It might be a regular family supper, sharing special occasions, or taking part in yearly activities that are important to your family. These customs foster a feeling of identity, bolster familial ties, and foster a sense of collective belonging.

• **Express Gratitude and Affection:** Healthy relationships depend on the expression of love and gratitude. Spend some time telling your adult child how much you value them.

Give them specific comments, acknowledge their accomplishments, and thank them for being in your life. Small acts of kindness, like sending a sincere message, leaving a note, or surprising them with a meaningful present, can go a long way towards fostering your relationship and reaffirming your love for one another.

# Suggestions for creating meaningful traditions, fostering shared interests, and maintaining regular communication

It takes care and work from both parties to maintain the special and developing dynamic that exists between parents and their adult children.

It becomes increasingly important to discover ways to retain close ties, cultivate common interests, and create meaningful traditions when children grow into adults and set off on their own travels. We will look at some ideas in this post for fostering these relationships and improving communication between parents and their adult children.

Acceptance of new traditions is important because they help families bond. It's crucial to accept new traditions that take into account the shifting dynamics of the family, even while certain traditions may inevitably change as kids get older. Talk about the traditions you want to keep, change, or start as a family over dinner. It might be a regular game night, a family vacation every year, or even a special meal that everyone pitches in to prepare. You may make sure that the traditions have meaning for each family member and build the relationship between parents and adult children by including everyone in the decision-making process.

**Participate in Activities You Both Enjoy**

Finding shared hobbies or interests might help parents and adult children stay in touch regularly. This can entail engaging in shared hobbies like hiking, cooking, painting, or even enrolling in a class.

To attempt new things that fascinate your older children, be willing to venture outside of your comfort zone and promote open-mindedness. By participating in activities that you both enjoy, you not only make time for bonding possible but also demonstrate your sincere interest in and support of one another's hobbies.

## Make Regular Communication a Priority

Keeping in touch regularly is essential to fostering a solid relationship between parents and adult children. The development of technology has made it simpler than ever to stay connected.

Use a variety of communication methods to check in frequently, including phone calls, video chats, emails, and even text messages. Make it a practice to catch up, talk about important issues, and share updates about your lives. Consider holding frequent family get-togethers or meetings, either in person or digitally, to create a special setting for honest conversation and closeness.

## Plan Milestones and Special Occasions

Together, commemorate anniversaries and memorable moments to make enduring memories. Make an effort to spend time together as a family on holidays, birthdays, anniversaries, and other special occasions. Plan social events or enjoyable activities for all, and include your adult children in the planning process to ensure their preferences are taken into account. By recognizing and celebrating these important occasions, you show how important family is to you and strengthen the bond between parents and grown children.

## Foster Intergenerational Learning

The chance for intergenerational learning is one of the special advantages of the parent-adult-child relationship. Parents may impart a lot of wisdom and life experience, and older children can offer new viewpoints and ideas.

Promote discussion of concepts, viewpoints, and experiences. Discuss in-depth issues that concern both parties and pay close attention to one another's points of view. You may enhance your relationship while also fostering mutual growth and understanding by encouraging intergenerational learning.

Understand that adult children may have different routes, values, and objectives than their parents. Respect individual paths. Even if their decisions go against your expectations or ideas, you must respect and encourage them.

Do not impose your opinions or pressure others to follow your wishes. Instead, promote a welcoming and understanding environment. Show a sincere interest in their endeavors, engage them in conversation, and pay attention to their points of view. You show them your unwavering love and give them a safe place to be themselves by honoring their distinct paths.

## Accept Technology and Social Media

In the current digital era, technology, and social media websites can be useful instruments for maintaining connections. Make use of these platforms to reduce the physical gap between parents and adult children. Share updates, pictures, and memories on social media. Comment on, like, and support one other's online endeavors to interact with each other's online presence. Additionally, look into tech-related activities with your family, such as online gaming, virtual book clubs, or even taking online classes. You can come up with creative strategies to promote common interests and keep in touch by adjusting to new technologies.

## Plan Family Getaways or Reunions

As a chance for everyone to get together in a casual and pleasurable setting, think about planning recurring family getaways or reunions. These retreats can be hosted in a rented cabin, a favorite family vacation place, or even a location that has special meaning for the family. Allowing for the participation of each family member will help to ensure that there is something enjoyable for everyone. These get-togethers improve relationships, give valuable face-to-face time, and produce priceless memories that will last a lifetime.

# Conclusion

It takes a careful balancing act of recognition, understanding, and communication to cross generational gaps and develop healthy connections with adult offspring. Understanding the changing dynamics between parents and adult children is crucial because it enables us to understand the need for boundaries and the desire for independence.

Parents can develop enduring relationships with their adult children by encouraging open channels of communication, exhibiting empathy, and upholding mutual respect. Even though the path may be difficult at times, the rewards of forging deep connections across generational divides are immense, laying a foundation of love, trust, and support that can stand the test of time.